3

Let's go to the zoo!
Allons au zoo!

Isabella was going to the zoo with the neighbours' children. She was looking at a plan of the zoo and deciding which order to see the animals in.

"Yes," she thought. "We'll see 'les **zèbres**', the zebras, 'les **girafes**', the giraffes, 'les **kangourous**', the kangaroos, and then 'les **éléphants**', the elephants. We can then have a quick snack before going to see 'les **pingouins**', the penguins, 'les **tigres**', the tigers, 'les **lions**', the lions, and 'les **hippopotames**', the hippopotamuses – all before lunch."

There was one animal on the plan that she didn't know, so she asked Max, the butler, "what's an '**ours blanc**'?"

"An 'ours' is a bear," replied Max, the butler, "and 'blanc' means 'white'."

"Ah, a polar bear!" declared Isabella. "Well, we'll definitely see it and then we can go on to 'les **gorilles**', the gorillas. '**Chameaux**? Chameaux?' – oh – , camels. It does sound a bit like English when you say it often enough. What's an '**autruche**' though?"

"That's an ostrich," replied Max, the butler.

"Oh yes, and the '**serpents**' must be the snakes," said Isabella. "I'm completely stuck with the '**singes**' though."

"That's the monkeys, of course," replied Max, the butler. "You'll have to visit them, what with the neighbours' children being such little monkeys themselves!"

Which are 'les singes'?

SINGES

4

Find the animals

Find the names of the five animals hidden in this wordsearch.

a	b	c	d	a	e	f	g	h	i	j	k
l	m	h	o	u	r	s	b	l	a	n	c
o	p	i	q	t	r	s	t	u	v	w	x
y	t	i	g	r	e	i	a	a	b	b	c
l	i	o	n	u	d	n	e	f	f	g	g
z	h	n	j	c	j	g	k	f	t	x	n
m	m	n	o	h	p	e	q	w	e	p	g
z	è	b	r	e	s	t	s	t	u	v	w

Top Tips

Most of the French **nouns** for these animals are **masculine** – regardless of whether the animal itself is male or female – so 'a' is therefore '**un**'. Only '**une** girafe' and 'une autruche' are **feminine**.

Did you know?

The word for the camel's 'hump' is 'la bosse'. You also use this word for a 'bump' on the head. The English word 'embossed' means something is 'raised above the surface' (often writing or a picture). In other words, if something is embossed, it sticks up like the camel's hump.

Bingo!
Loto!

Sir Ralph Witherbottom had invented a Bingo machine that calls out numbers. Max, the butler, had helped him to put the numbers into French and now they are trying out the machine with Isabella. A fun afternoon of French Bingo!

"**Quarante-neuf**!" called the machine.

Isabella crossed 49 off her card.

"**Cinquante-sept**!" called the machine.

Sir Ralph was looking hot and bothered.

Erm...Loto

"'Quarante' is 'forty' and 'cinquante' is 'fifty'," Max reminded him.

"Oh yes, of course – 57," said Sir Ralph. His eyes lit up as he crossed it off his card.

"**Quarante et un, cinquante-trois, quarante-deux**!" called the machine, faster this time.

Isabella quickly crossed 41 and 53 off her card. Max, the butler, crossed 42 off his.

"**Quarante-trois, cinquante-huit, cinquante-quatre**," were the next lot of numbers.

Sir Ralph crossed off 43 and 58. Isabella had 54.

"**Trente-six, trente-sept, soixante**!" called the machine. "**Trente-huit, cinquante-neuf, quarante-cinq**." It seemed that something was not quite right. The Bingo machine was going much too fast.

"36, 37, 60," muttered Max, concentrating hard. "38, 59, 45." Sir Ralph Witherbottom and Isabella could not keep up and were getting a bit flustered.

Soon it was going so fast that even Max couldn't keep up. Then there was a loud 'bang' and nuts, bolts, springs and cogs flew through the air. That was the end of the Bingo machine!

"It's back to the drawing board for this invention then!" laughed Sir Ralph.

Which card wins?

Work out which card will win, by crossing off the numbers on all of the cards as the machine calls them out.

B	I	N	G	O	
30	32	43	47	50	51

B	I	N	G	O	
31	32	44	48	51	60

B	I	N	G	O	
32	33	45	49	53	59

The machine calls out:

Trente

Trente-deux

Quarante-quatre

Quarante-neuf

Cinquante-trois

Cinquante-neuf

Quarante-trois

Quarante-sept

Cinquante

Cinquante et un

Top Tips

Once you know the numbers for twenty, thirty, forty, fifty and sixty in French, as well as your numbers from one to twenty, you can work out sixty-nine numbers.

Did you know?

You can put the letters 'aine' onto the end of a number in French to make it mean a quantity of 'about that many'. For example, 'une quarantaine' means 'about forty', and 'une trentaine' means 'about thirty'. Our word 'dozen' comes from the French, 'une douzaine' – 'about twelve'.

It's holiday time!
Vive les vacances!

Isabella was studying the calendar in the hallway.

"Isn't the French year busy?" she said to Max, the butler. "So, they call New Year's Day, 'le Jour de l'An'. Christmas is 'Noël', I see. 'La Veille de Noël' must be Christmas Eve.

"Someone has written the word 'Réveillon' on the day before 'le Jour de l'An' and 'la Veille de Noël'. What does that mean?" asked Isabella.

"That's the traditional meal that's eaten quite late in the evening on both days – often not until midnight," explained Max, the butler.

"So what's 'Mardi Gras', in February?" asked Isabella.

"Fat Tuesday," said Max, the butler. "Pancake Day."

"Good, I love pancakes!" said Isabella. 'Mercredi des Cendres' must be Ash Wednesday then. 'Pâques' must be Easter, as it's a Sunday in April. Someone has written 'oeufs en chocolat' two days before that. Oh, I know what they are – chocolate eggs, of course. Yum!"

Mardi Gras and Pâques are my favourites!

"'La Fête des Mères' is Mother's Day," said Max, the butler. "May is a good month for holidays. There's 'la Fête du Travail', the workers' holiday, on the first of May, 'le Jour de l'Ascension', Ascension Day, and 'Pentecôte', Whitsun."

"What's this on the fourteenth of July?" asked Isabella.

"Ah," said Max, the butler. "'La Fête Nationale' – the biggest bank holiday in France. No one will work that day. There'll be parades, dancing, street parties and fireworks. Ah, and look what the housekeeper has written in, two days after that – 'les noces de Marie'! Her sister, Marie, is getting married!"

Which celebration?

Join the picture to the correct celebration.

Noël

Pâques

La Fête des Mères

Mardi Gras

La Fête Nationale

Top Tips!

Some days in calendars or timetables are marked as 'ponts' – bridges. This is an extra day's holiday added between a bank holiday and a weekend to make a longer holiday.

Did you know?

The French Revolution started on the 14th July 1789. Crowds broke into a prison, the Bastille, and let out all the prisoners. The Bastille held people who had not had a trial, and this was seen as royal unfairness. This day, 'La Fête Nationale', sometimes also called Bastille Day, is celebrated every year in France. It is the most important French holiday.

Revise Time

1 Circle the names of five animals.

SINGEZÈBRELIONOURSBLANCTIGRE

2 Three of these animals are masculine (m). Two are feminine (f). Write 'm' or 'f' next to each one.

a Serpent _____

b Pingouin _____

c Girafe _____

d Autruche _____

e Chameau _____

3 Here are some sums in French. First, write the answer in numerals, then in French.

a soixante – cinquante-deux = _____
   [   ] – [   ]

b quarante-trois – trente et un = _____
   [   ] – [   ]

c cinquante – quarante-neuf = _____
   [   ] – [   ]

d cinquante-neuf – trente-trois = _____
   [   ] – [   ]

e quarante-neuf – quarante-quatre = _____
   [   ] – [   ]

4 Put a ring round the numbers that contain a 3 when written as numerals. It may help to write them down first.

trente-trois   quarante-quatre   cinquante-cinq   soixante

trente et un   quarante-cinq   cinquante-six   cinquante-neuf

trente-quatre   trente-deux   quarante-six   cinquante-sept

quarante-huit   cinquante-trois   cinquante-sept

5 Draw a line between the French festival and the month it is in.

a Noël   January

b La Fête des Mères   July

c La Fête du Travail   December

d La Fête Nationale   May

e Le Jour de l'An   May

6 Fill in the missing letters to spell out the names of some of the French festivals. Write next to them what they mean in English.

a L _ V _ i _ l _ d _ N _ ë _   _____

b P _ q _ e _   _____

c M _ r _ i _ r _ s   _____

d P _ n _ e _ ô _ e   _____

                                     _____

e L _ J _ u _ d _ l' _ s _ e _ s _ o _

11

What's the time, Mr Wolf?
Quelle heure est-il, Monsieur Le Loup?

Isabella and Max were thinking of ideas for games they could play with the little village children on 'la Fête'.

"Well, there's always, 'What's the time, Mr Wolf?'" suggested Max. "**Quelle heure est-il**, Monsieur Le Loup?"

Max explained how the game worked – she asks him the time, he replies, then she takes that number of steps towards him. At some point though, he won't say a time, but instead will tell her it is time to eat her up and come chasing after her!

Isabella decided to try the game and said to Max, "Quelle heure est-il, Monsieur Le loup?"

"**Il est une heure**," replied Max.

Isabella took one step forward.

"Il est deux heures," said Max.

Isabella took two steps.

"Il est trois heures," said Max.

Il est midi. C'est l'heure de te manger!

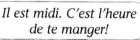

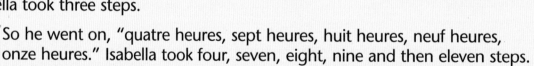

Isabella took three steps.

So he went on, "quatre heures, sept heures, huit heures, neuf heures, onze heures." Isabella took four, seven, eight, nine and then eleven steps.

"Il est onze heures **et quart**," said Max. Isabella took eleven and a quarter steps.

Next Max said, "onze heures **et demie**" and then, "**midi moins le quart**."

Isabella took eleven and a half and then eleven and three quarter steps. She had got to the other end of the room and Max was just in front of her. He turned round and jumped at her.

"C'est midi! C'est l'heure de te manger! It's midday. Time to eat you up!" he shouted.

Isabella giggled and ran away from Max, pretending to be scared.

A game of 'What's the time, Mr Wolf?'

Starting on the flagstone marked on the garden path, play 'Quelle heure est-il, Monsieur Le Loup?'. Mark where you will land after each time 'Monsieur Le Loup' calls out, counting each flagstone as one step. Where do you end up?

Il est cinq heures.

Il est trois heures.

Il est six heures.

Il est sept heures.

Il est une heure.

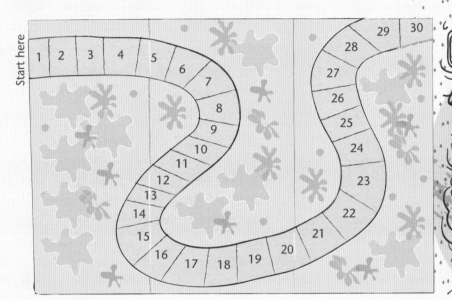

You may say 'twelve o'clock' in four ways. 'Midi' means twelve noon, 'minuit' means midnight, 'zéro heure' is midnight and 'douze heures' is midday.

Did you know?

'Quarter past two' in French, is really 'two hours and quarter' – 'deux heures et quart'. 'Half past' is really 'and half' – 'et demie'. 'Quarter to' is 'minus the quarter' – 'moins le quart'. If you know all of this, your numbers and the three other ways of saying 'twelve o'clock', you can say fifty-seven different times!

Morning, afternoon and night
Le matin, l'après-midi et le soir

1	Nuit
2	
3	
4	
5	
6	
7	
8	Matin
9	
10	
11	
Noon	Midi
1	
2	
3	Après-midi
4	
5	
6	Soir
7	
8	
9	
10	
11	Nuit
Midnight	Minuit

Isabella was always making mistakes when she arranged meetings with her new French friends – she kept getting the part of the day slightly wrong.

"Will you help me?" she asked Max.

"Of course," said Max. "Now let me see. '**Tôt**' is very early; early in any circumstances. When you mean it as part of a day, that would be early morning – before seven."

"Then there's '**de bonne heure**' – another way of saying 'tôt' and, word for word, means 'of good time'. It's a bit like our 'in good time'. So, if you're talking about when you get up, it would mean, about seven. That would give you plenty of time!" Max continued.

"So when is '**le matin**'?" asked Isabella.

"Let's make a chart, so I can show you. Now, write 'le matin' on there for morning, so that takes us to lunchtime. When your friends say they'll meet you at '**midi**', they really mean lunchtime, even though that actually means midday. 'Midi' could be any time from half past eleven until when lunch is over, which could be as late as half past two," Max continued.

Mmm. I don't think I'll be asking Bernadette to come 'tôt' for breakfast. I like my sleep too much!

"So '**après-midi**' is from when lunch is finished until …?" said Isabella, as she filled in her chart.

"Well, all afternoon until just before dinner – six o'clock, perhaps," said Max.

"I know '**soir**' comes next – the evening," said Isabella.

"Yes, until you go to bed, when the '**nuit**', night, begins. Then, if you have a midnight feast, that would be at '**minuit**'!" said Max.

Which time of day is this?

Join the descriptions to the time of day.

Before breakfast  Midi

Before midday  L'après-midi

After lunch  La nuit

While you're asleep  Le matin

At lunchtime  Tôt

Top Tips

When giving the time, specify the part of the day;
'du matin' – in the morning, 'de l'après-midi' – in
the afternoon, and 'du soir' – in the evening.

Did you know?

We use the French word 'matinee' (notice the accent is missing) when
talking about an afternoon performance of a play, pantomime or
ballet. In French, though, 'matinée' still refers to the morning. 'Faire la
grasse matinée' means 'to make a fat morning' or, in other words, 'to
have a lie-in'!

Same old routine
Le train-train

The Witherbottoms' housekeeper was in bed with the flu. Isabella was helping Max to do all of the chores. Max was reading the list that the housekeeper had given him.

6.00 Je me réveille

"So, she wakes up at six," said Max.

6.15 Je me lève et je me douche

"She gets up and has her shower at 6.15.

6.30 Je nettoie la cuisine

She cleans the kitchen at 6.30.

7.00 Je prépare le petit déjeuner

She gets the breakfast ready at 7.00.

8.00 Je fais les lits

She makes the beds at 8.00.

8.30 Je fais la vaisselle

She does the washing up at 8.30. Gosh, she does a lot," he remarked.

9.00 – 11.00 Je passe l'aspirateur

"Then, between 9.00 and 11.00 she hoovers,

Je range le salon et la salle à manger

tidies the lounge and the dining room,

Je nettoie la salle de bains

and cleans the bathroom.

11.00 Je prépare le déjeuner

Next, at 11.00, she prepares the lunch.

13.30 Je fais la vaisselle

After we've eaten, she washes up.

14.30 Je fais le repassage

Then, finally, she does the ironing. Phew!"

Goodness! Eleven already. Should I be making lunch or washing up?!

"Wow, and it's already 9am!" said Max. "We'd better get a move on, Izzy."

Muddled-up routines

Unscramble these words to work out the tasks that you need to do.

1 | eJ sapse asteul'rapir

_____

2 | eJ safi al vealilses

_____

3 | eJ safi sel stil

_____

4 | eJ perépar el jéunerde

_____

5 | eJ ganer el noals

_____

Top Tips

'Je *me* réveille', 'je *me* lève' and 'je *me* douche' are
examples of reflexive verbs in French. They are called
this, because you do these actions *to yourself*.

Did you know?

'Je fais' is used in many expressions. It means 'I do' or 'I make'. So, in the
examples you have just read, the housekeeper 'does' the washing up and
the ironing, but 'makes' the beds. You will also find that you 'do' horse
riding, skiing, swimming and jogging, but you 'make' a snowman.

Revise Time

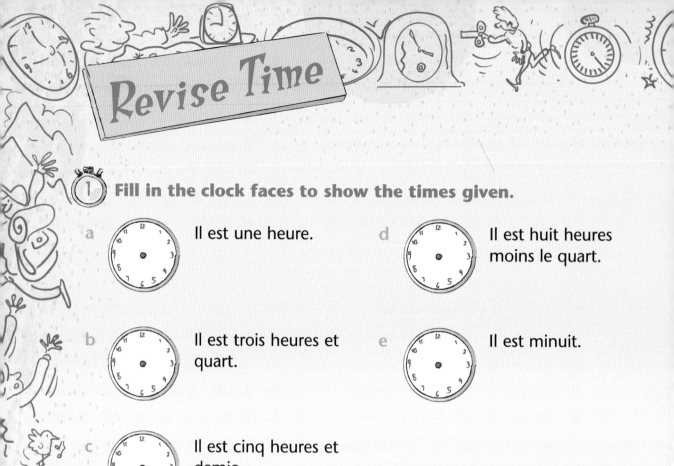

1 **Fill in the clock faces to show the times given.**

a Il est une heure.

d Il est huit heures moins le quart.

b Il est trois heures et quart.

e Il est minuit.

c Il est cinq heures et demie.

2 **Write 'vrai' (true) or 'faux' (false) next to each statement.**

a Il est deux heures et quart.

_____

c Il est sept heures et demie.

_____

b Il est une heure et quart.

_____

d Il est deux heures et demie.

_____

3 **Fill in the missing letters to make the words for a particular time of day.**

a _ e _ o _ n _ h _ u _ e

d m _ t _ n

b m _ d _

e a _ r _ s - m _ d _

c s _ i _

18

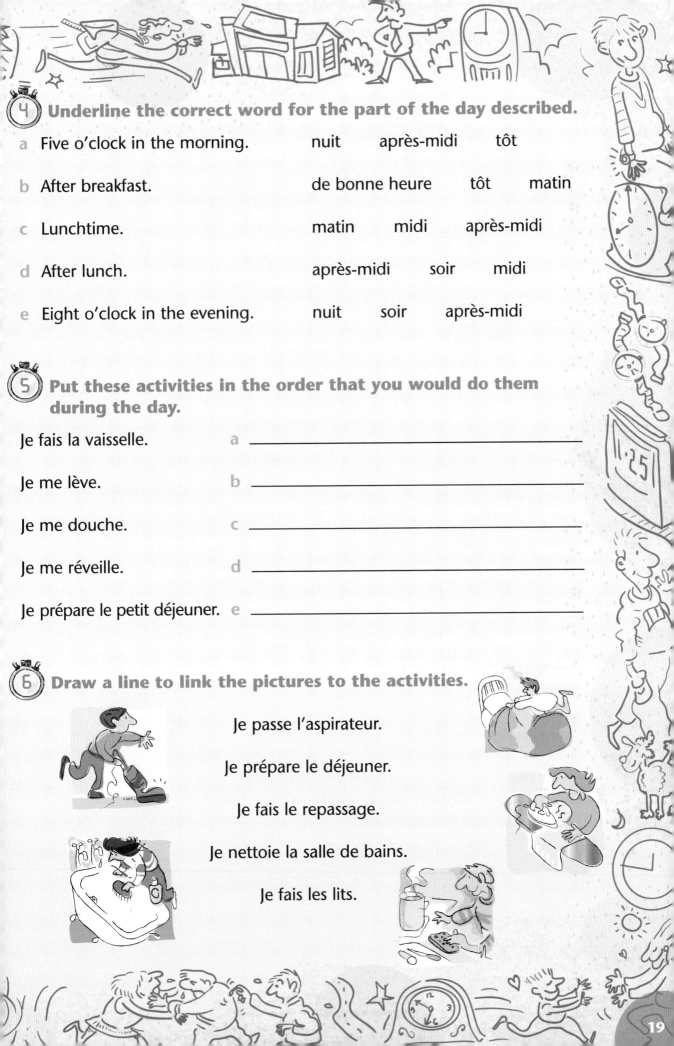

4 Underline the correct word for the part of the day described.

a Five o'clock in the morning.   nuit   après-midi   tôt

b After breakfast.   de bonne heure   tôt   matin

c Lunchtime.   matin   midi   après-midi

d After lunch.   après-midi   soir   midi

e Eight o'clock in the evening.   nuit   soir   après-midi

5 Put these activities in the order that you would do them during the day.

Je fais la vaisselle.   a _____

Je me lève.   b _____

Je me douche.   c _____

Je me réveille.   d _____

Je prépare le petit déjeuner.   e _____

6 Draw a line to link the pictures to the activities.

Je passe l'aspirateur.

Je prépare le déjeuner.

Je fais le repassage.

Je nettoie la salle de bains.

Je fais les lits.

A strange way of counting
Des nombres bizarres

"I just don't understand these numbers," said Sir Ralph.

He was looking through phone numbers of firms who might be able to supply him with parts for one of his new inventions.

"I mean, '**soixante-dix**' – surely that means sixty-ten. You don't say 'sixty-ten'," he continued. "It should be seventy!"

"Ah, but it's different in French," said Max. "The numbers go 'soixante-dix', '**soixante et onze**', seventy-one, '**soixante-douze**', seventy-two, '**soixante-treize**', seventy-three, '**soixante-quatorze**', seventy-four, '**soixante-quinze**', seventy-five, '**soixante-seize**', seventy-six, '**soixante-dix-sept**', seventy-seven, '**soixante-dix-huit**', seventy-eight, and '**soixante-dix-neuf**', seventy-nine."

Quatre-vingt-dix-neuf – four twenties are eighty, add ten, that's ninety, add nine – makes ninety-nine.

"What about this as well?" asked Sir Ralph. "'**Quatre-vingt-trois**'? That's 'four twenty-three'. Surely it should be 'eighty-three'?"

"'**Quatre-vingts**' is indeed the word for 'eighty' in French," said Max, "and what's more, 'ninety' is '**quatre-vingt-dix**', and so it goes on, '**quatre-vingt-onze**', ninety-one, '**quatre-vingt-douze**', ninety-two… and then you get to '**cent**', one hundred."

"Well, I'd better practise my arithmetic then," said Sir Ralph.

A hidden telephone number

Cross out the numerals in the box that match the numbers written in words. The three numerals left over, when put in the correct order, starting with the lowest and ending with the highest, make the mystery number.

soixante-dix	quatre-vingt-dix-neuf
quatre-vingt-dix-huit	quatre-vingt-sept
soixante-douze	soixante-quinze
quatre-vingt-dix-sept	quatre-vingt-seize
quatre-vingt-quinze	quatre-vingt-douze
soixante-dix-neuf	quatre-vingts
quatre-vingt-un	quatre-vingt-trois
quatre-vingt-cinq	

```
   70        87
          96     91
      90      79
          72     92
   85    98
              80
          75
   99          97
          81
              83
   89
              95
```

Mystery telephone number = _____

Top Tips!

French telephone numbers are usually written out in twos, for example 71 74 83. You say 'soixante et onze, soixante-quatorze, quatre-vingt-trois'.

Did you know?

The bizarre way of counting, 'soixante-dix, soixante et onze', then 'quatre-vingts', 'quatre-vingt-dix' was originally used as a secret code in France to show which side you were on between two rival families. The family who chose to count in the peculiar way gained more friends than the other family, so we are left with such numbers as 'quatre-vingt-dix-neuf'.

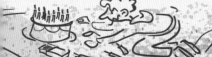

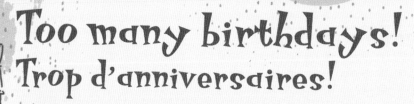

Too many birthdays!
Trop d'anniversaires!

One of Isabella's friends wished her 'Bon **anniversaire**' – Happy Birthday.

She gave her a beautiful book, in which Isabella could write people's birthdays.

Isabella asked all her friends when their birthdays were.

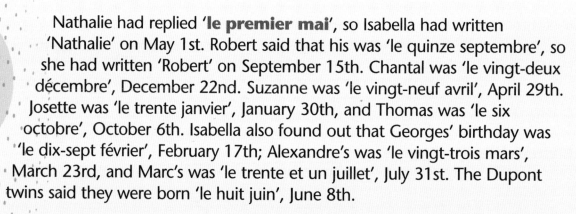

"**C'est quand, ton anniversaire**?" she said, which means 'When is your birthday?'

Nathalie had replied '**le premier mai**', so Isabella had written 'Nathalie' on May 1st. Robert said that his was 'le quinze septembre', so she had written 'Robert' on September 15th. Chantal was 'le vingt-deux décembre', December 22nd. Suzanne was 'le vingt-neuf avril', April 29th. Josette was 'le trente janvier', January 30th, and Thomas was 'le six octobre', October 6th. Isabella also found out that Georges' birthday was 'le dix-sept février', February 17th; Alexandre's was 'le vingt-trois mars', March 23rd, and Marc's was 'le trente et un juillet', July 31st. The Dupont twins said they were born 'le huit juin', June 8th.

> It'll be a social whirlwind with all these birthday parties!!!

Then Marc had said, "Et ma **fête**, c'est le vingt-neuf août."

"That can't be right. He's already told me his birthday is the 31st of July. He can't have two birthdays."

"You see, French people do have two special days;" said Max, "an 'anniversaire' and a 'fête'. French people have a saint's name as a middle name. On that saint's day, the French celebrate just as if it were their birthday. They have a party and their friends bring them presents and cards. They call this day their 'fête'."

Sorting out birthdays

Work out when the birthdays of five more of Isabella's friends are.

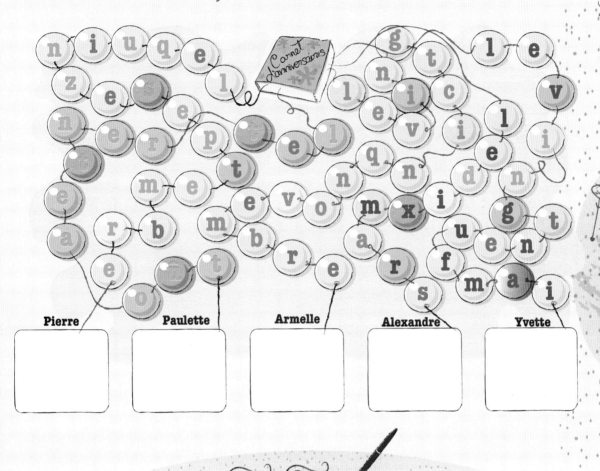

Pierre

Paulette

Armelle

Alexandre

Yvette

Top Tips

'Bon anniversaire **à toi**' means 'Happy Birthday to you'. 'Dear Izzy' is 'chère Izzy' and 'dear Pierre' is '**cher** Pierre'. The French often sing 'Happy Birthday' in English, though!

Did you know?

A French person's 'fête', – their saint's day – used to be considered even more important than their 'anniversaire', which marks the day on which they were born. French families no longer have to give their children a saint's name, but many still choose to do so. The 'fête' is often more of a family celebration and the 'anniversaire' is more for friends, though very close friends and relations will attend both.

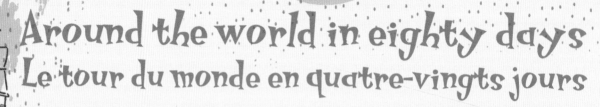

Around the world in eighty days
Le tour du monde en quatre-vingts jours

Isabella had just finished reading a fantastic adventure story called 'Le tour du monde en quatre-vingts jours' – 'Around the world in eighty days', in which Phileas Fogg and his companion Passepartout set out to travel round the whole of the world in eighty days.

Isabella realised that her geography was not very good, as she did not know where most of the places were that Mr Fogg visited. She decided to make herself a list in English of as many continents, countries, seas, rivers and mountain ranges as she could think of. Then she looked them up in her French atlas and added the French names to the list too.

Continents
Continents

Africa
Afrique (f)
America
Amérique (f)
Asia
Asie (f)
Europe
Europe (f)

Countries
Pays

Australia
Australie (f)
Canada
Canada (m)
China
Chine (f)
France
France (f)
Germany
Allemagne (f)
Great Britain
Grande-Bretagne (f)
India
Inde (f)
Italy
Italie (f)
Japan
Japon (m)
The Netherlands
Pays-Bas (m pl)
New Zealand
Nouvelle Zélande (f)
Scandinavia
Scandinavie (f)
Spain
Espagne (f)
Switzerland
Suisse (f)
The United States
Les États-Unis (m pl)

Rivers
Fleuves

Ganges
Gange (m)
Loire
Loire (f)
Nile
Nil (m)
Seine
Seine (f)
Thames
Tamise (f)

> We ought to be on our way back to London by now.

Seas
Mers

Atlantic
Atlantique (m)
The Channel
Manche (f)
Pacific
Pacifique (m)

Mountain Ranges
Chaînes de Montagnes

Alps
Alpes (pl)
Himalayas
Himalaya (m)
Pyrenees
Pyrénées (pl)
Rockies
Rocheuses (pl)

Geographical wheel

Find one river, one mountain range, one continent, two countries and one sea hidden in this wheel.

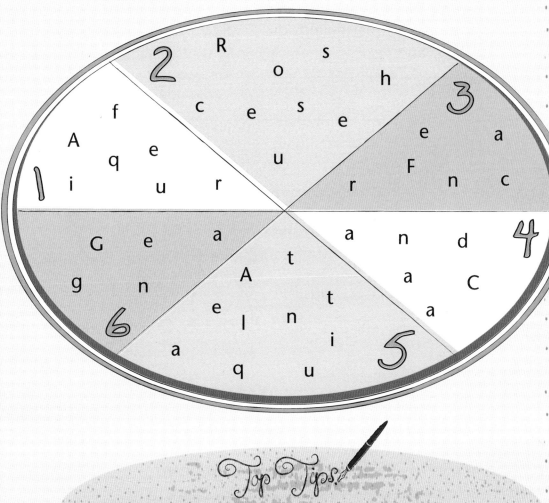

Top Tips

'En' means 'to' or 'in' a **feminine** (f) country or continent, 'au' is used for **masculine** (m) and 'aux' for plurals (pl).

Did you know?

Jules Verne was a well-known French author. He wrote many exciting adventure stories, which were translated into other languages and made into films. These include 'Journey to the Centre of the Earth', 'Twenty Thousand Leagues Under the Sea', 'The Mysterious Island', 'From Earth to Moon', 'Round the Moon' and, of course, 'Around the World in Eighty Days'.

Revise Time

1 **Make as many numbers as you can by joining any two or more of these together.**

soixante   quatre-vingt-dix   dix   sept   huit

_____

_____

_____

2 **Match the words to the numbers by drawing a line between them.**

80   83

99

a Soixante-quatorze   d Quatre-vingt-dix-neuf

65   74

b Soixante-cinq   e Quatre-vingt-trois

c Quatre-vingts

3 **Answer these questions.**

a If someone says it is their 'fête', what do they mean?

_____

b How do you say 'Happy Birthday' in French?

_____

c What does 'C'est quand, ton anniversaire?' mean in English?

_____

d How do you say 'dear Izzy' in French?

_____

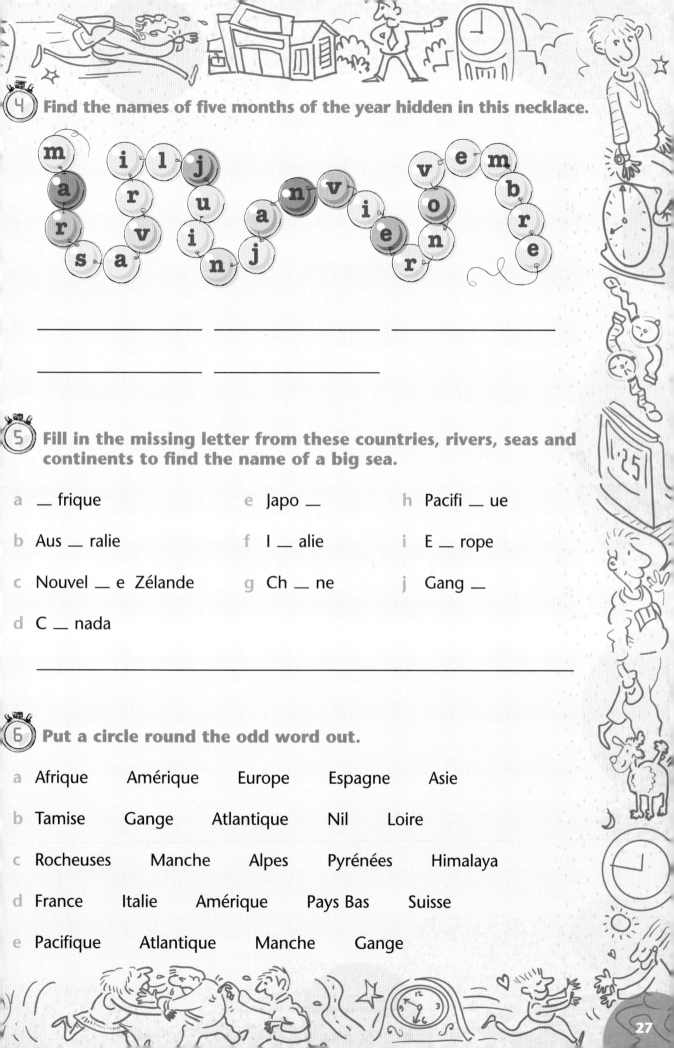

4 Find the names of five months of the year hidden in this necklace.

_____ _____ _____

_____ _____

5 Fill in the missing letter from these countries, rivers, seas and continents to find the name of a big sea.

a __ frique

b Aus __ ralie

c Nouvel __ e Zélande

d C __ nada

e Japo __

f I __ alie

g Ch __ ne

h Pacifi __ ue

i E __ rope

j Gang __

_____

6 Put a circle round the odd word out.

a Afrique   Amérique   Europe   Espagne   Asie

b Tamise   Gange   Atlantique   Nil   Loire

c Rocheuses   Manche   Alpes   Pyrénées   Himalaya

d France   Italie   Amérique   Pays Bas   Suisse

e Pacifique   Atlantique   Manche   Gange

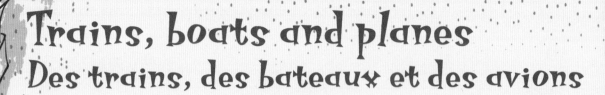

Trains, boats and planes
Des trains, des bateaux et des avions

Sir Ralph had decided he would like to do a week's tour of Europe, so he asked Max to ring the travel agent and ask them to put together an itinerary.

Lundi, en avion de Paris à Genève.

"They suggested you go by plane from Paris to Geneva on Monday," said Max.

Mardi, par le **train** de Genève à Mayence, en **Allemagne**.

"Then by train to Mainz, in Germany, on Tuesday.

Mercredi, en **bateau** sur le Rhin de Mayence à Cologne.

Wednesday, by boat on the Rhine to Cologne.

Jeudi, en **voiture** de Cologne à Amsterdam, au Pays Bas.

On to Amsterdam, in the Netherlands, by car on Thursday.

Vendredi, tour d'Amsterdam à **vélo**.

A bike tour of Amsterdam on Friday.

De Amsterdam à Bruxelles, en **Belgique**, en **autobus**.

Amsterdam to Brussels, in Belgium, by bus.

Samedi, prendre le **tramway** jusqu'à l'aéroport.

Saturday, take the tram to the airport.

En **Italie** en avion de Belgique.

Then on to Italy by plane.

Dimanche, **randonnée à pied** dans les montagnes.

Sunday, hiking in the mountains.

Lundi, **retour** à Paris en avion.

Monday, return to Paris by plane.

All sounds a bit hectic to me, sir!"

"Nonsense, it sounds splendid!" said Sir Ralph, who always did like a challenge.

It's Friday, so this must be Amsterdam.

Tour of Europe crossword

Read the clues and fill in the answers in French.

Verticalement

1 Wednesday

3 Italy

Horizontalement

2 By train

4 Boat

5 Plane

You travel 'en' or 'à' a kind of transport. You can only
use 'en' if you actually travel inside it. So, it's 'en
voiture', but 'à vélo'. One exception is 'par le train'.

Did you know?

The French say they are going away for 'huit jours', eight days, when
they go away for a week. Similarly, they say 'quinze jours', fifteen days,
for a fortnight. This is because you tend to go and come back on the
same weekday. So, that's eight or fifteen days when you're not at home
for a whole day.

Let's go!
On y va!

Ouf! Next time, je vais prendre l'ascenseur!

Isabella had received an email from her French friend Jeanne. She asked Max to help her understand it.

"'**Je vais** à la Tour Eiffel demain'," read Max. "Oh, she's saying, 'I'm going to the Eiffel Tower tomorrow'. '**Tu vas** venir aussi?' and she's asking, 'Are you going to come as well?' Marc, '**il va** monter l'escalier à pied et maman, **elle va** prendre l'ascenseur', he's going to go up the stairs on foot and their mum is going to take the lift. '**Nous allons** voir tout Paris du sommet'. 'We're going to see all of Paris from the top'. 'Sir Ralph et toi, **vous allez** venir **chez nous** à deux heures?' So, 'you and Sir Ralph are going to come to our house at two o'clock?' 'Papa et Sir Ralph, **ils vont aller** en ville.' Her dad and Sir Ralph are going to go into town. 'Mes deux sœurs, **elles vont aller** à la piscine,' and her two sisters are going to the swimming pool."

"Yes, I think I understand all of that now," said Isabella, reading through the email again.

> Je vais à la Tour Eiffel demain. Tu vas venir aussi? Marc, il va monter à pied et maman, elle va prendre l'ascenseur. Nous allons voir tout Paris du sommet. Sir Ralph et toi, vous allez venir chez nous à deux heures? Papa et Sir Ralph, ils vont aller en ville. Mes deux sœurs, elles vont aller à la piscine.
>
> À bientôt,
>
> Jeanne

'Going' scrambled

Unscramble the parts of the verb 'aller', 'to go', and match them with the correct pronoun.

Pronouns   je   tu   il   elle   nous   vous   ils   elles

Parts of 'aller'   tonv   sav   ivas   tnov   zelal   snolal   av   av

_____   _____   _____   _____

_____   _____   _____   _____

_____   _____   _____   _____

_____   _____   _____   _____

Top Tips

The 'il' and 'elle' parts of the verb **'aller'** are the same and so are the 'ils' and 'elles' parts. This happens with many French verbs.

Did you know?

All languages have verbs that don't follow a predictable pattern. French is no exception and for years people studying French have complained about the number of verbs they have had to learn. Even more unfortunately, these irregular verbs, like **'aller'**, are generally the ones that are used most often.

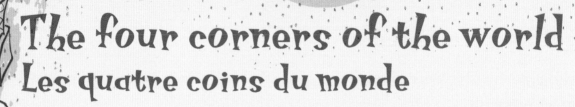

The four corners of the world
Les quatre coins du monde

Isabella was bored. She had been forced to stay in now for three days, because she had a cold. Now she was looking for something to amuse herself with in Sir Ralph's library.

She spun the large globe round. Then she noticed that the writing on it was in French.

"Oh, so '**nord**' means 'north', '**sud**' means 'south', '**est**' means 'east' and '**ouest**' means 'west'," she thought. "Not too difficult, really."

She looked for some other words she might recognise. She found '**île**', 'island', and '**océan**', 'ocean', which seemed very much like English. Then there were some other words she recognised, because she had seen them before – '**montagnes**', 'mountains', and '**fleuves**', 'rivers'.

She then noticed a book Sir Ralph had left open on his desk and read, "Lille est une grande **ville** industrielle dans le nord de la France."

She tried to figure out what it meant. "'Lille … is … a … big … industrial … town in the north of France.' That wasn't too bad!" she thought. "Bordeaux est un **port** important dans le sud-ouest de la France," she read. "Easy! 'Bordeaux is an important port in the southwest of France.' Oh, but this is boring!"

She lay down on the sofa and closed her eyes.

> Izzy's retreat est une île importante dans le Pacifique sud.

Find out the name of the town

Use the letters in the box to create the French words for the English sentence below. Cross off each letter as you use it. The ones left will spell out the missing first word in the sentence – a mystery town!

N C E D N G E S N R E T E A D E V L U E S L D
A N S L E S U D L L R A E F R A E M I A I L

_____ is _ _ _

a _ _ _   big _ _ _ _ _ _   town _ _ _ _ _ _

in _ _ _ _   the _ _ south _ _ _

of _ _ _ _ _   France _ _ _ _ _ _ _.

Top Tips

We say 'le sud de la France' for 'the south of France', using the feminine 'the'. For masculine words, we use 'du', as in 'dans le nord du Portugal'.

Did you know?

The south of France is sometimes called the 'midi'. 'Midi' usually means 'midday' and can also mean 'south'. This is probably because the south coast of France directly faces the midday sun and the sun is directly above it at noon. The motorway, which leads there, is called the 'autoroute du soleil' – the sunshine motorway.

Revise Time

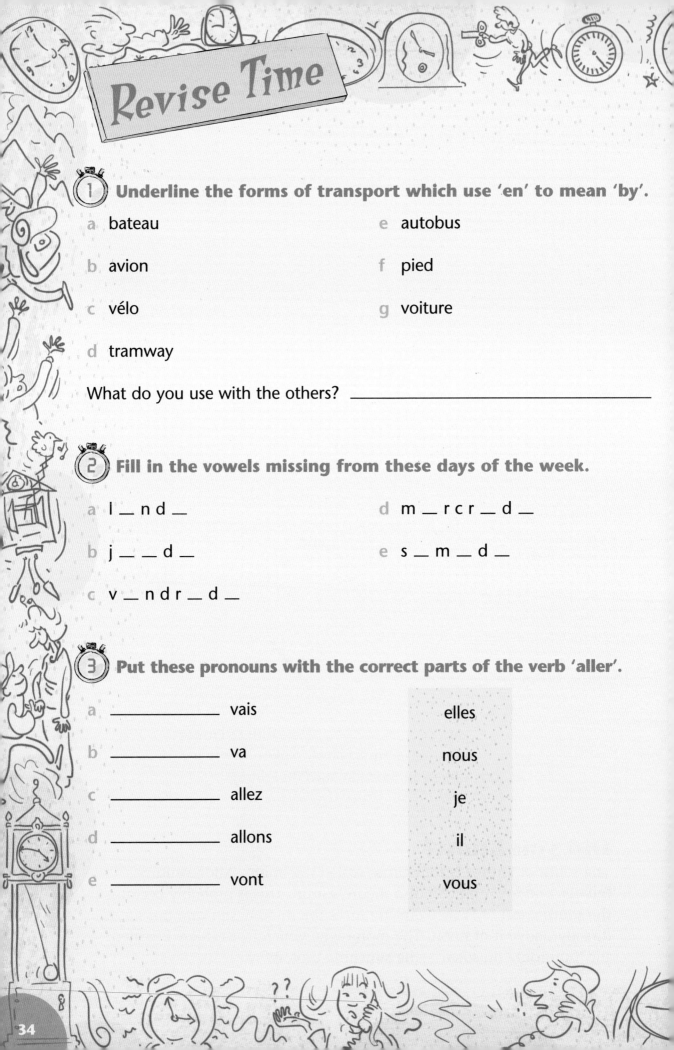

1 Underline the forms of transport which use 'en' to mean 'by'.

a bateau

b avion

c vélo

d tramway

e autobus

f pied

g voiture

What do you use with the others? _____

2 Fill in the vowels missing from these days of the week.

a l _ n d _

b j _ _ d _

c v _ n d r _ d _

d m _ r c r _ d _

e s _ m _ d _

3 Put these pronouns with the correct parts of the verb 'aller'.

a _____ vais

b _____ va

c _____ allez

d _____ allons

e _____ vont

elles

nous

je

il

vous

Write out what the following mean.

a Tu vas _____

b Elle va _____

c Nous allons _____

d Ils vont _____

e Je vais _____

5 **Cross out the words in colour which do not belong in each sentence.**

a Lille est une ville importante / un port important
   dans le nord / le sud de la France / l'Angleterre.

b Bordeaux est une grande ville / un grand port
   dans le sud-ouest / le nord-est de la France / l'Angleterre.

Use these two sentences to help you to write that Manchester is a big town in the north of England.

_____

_____

6 **Circle the odd one out.**

a est   nord   ouest   montagne

b fleuve   île   montagne   sud

c grand   industriel   important   port

d ouest   est   fleuve   nord

e océan   Pacifique   Lille   Bordeaux

The Tour de France
Le Tour de France

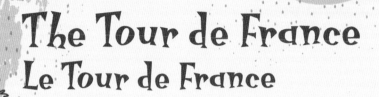

"Look at this map of the Tour de France, the famous French bike race, Izzy," Sir Ralph said, showing Isabella the map in the newspaper.

"The race starts in the capital, Paris," he said. "Then goes on to Le Mans, famous for motor racing."

"Next comes Poitiers, in a lovely countryside region known as 'la Vienne'," added Max. "Then it's on to La Rochelle on the west coast, then Biarritz on the Atlantic coast, not far from Spain, and Montpellier in the 'Midi' – all three very nice seaside towns."

"Next comes Cannes," said Sir Ralph, "where they hold the well-known film festival.

"Then they cycle on up to Annecy," continued Sir Ralph, "which isn't far from Switzerland. Afterwards, they go to Dijon, known for its mustard."

"Strasbourg comes next," said Max, "which is very close to Germany and has some street names which seem more German than French. The last stop, before they return to Paris, is Châlons-en-Champagne, near where they make champagne. Shall we turn on the radio to hear what's happening in the race?"

"L'Anglais **gagne**," said the radio.

Oh là là! Il est tombé!

"Oh, so the Englishman is winning," said Max.

"Non, il est **tombé**," said the radio.

"No, he's fallen," said Max.

"L'Espagnol a gagné," said the radio. "Il a le maillot jaune."

"The Spaniard's won!" exclaimed Max. "He has the yellow jersey. The winner of a day's stage – called 'étape' in French – always wears the yellow jersey the next day."

Bicycle wheels

Join the spare wheels to the bikes.

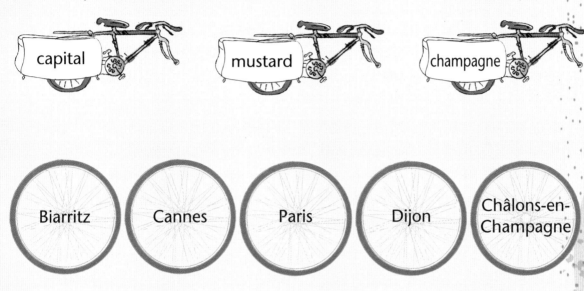

capital

mustard

champagne

Biarritz

Cannes

Paris

Dijon

Châlons-en-Champagne

films

seaside resort

Top Tips

The Tour de France takes place in July and features in our newspapers and on television. You will soon learn the names of many French towns if you follow it.

Did you know?

The Tour de France, divided into twenty 'étapes' or stages, goes through as many French 'départements' as possible. The 'départements' are a bit like our 'counties'. The Tour sometimes goes into other countries. It even came through the Channel Tunnel to Great Britain the year the tunnel opened.

Super-sleuth Sir Ralph Witherbottom
Super-détective Sir Ralph Witherbottom

"I get it!" shouted Sir Ralph one day. "Now I know why sometimes you put an 'e' on 'grand' for 'big' and sometimes you don't. It's all to do with **masculine** and **feminine**. Just like you have 'le' for 'the' for masculine words and 'la' for feminine ones. The 'e' is for feminine."

Max cleared his throat. "True, but if an **adjective** already ends in 'e'," he explained, "you don't need another one, like the French word for red, '**rouge**', for example."

"Or '**jaune**', yellow," added Sir Ralph, who was by then feeling extremely pleased with himself.

Max smiled and warned, "There are some, however, where the feminine is completely different from the masculine, like the word for good – '**bon**' and '**bonne**'."

"I think I'll write down all the ones I can find," said Sir Ralph and he started to make himself a chart.

word	masculine	feminine
big/tall	grand	grande
small	petit	petite
beautiful	beau	belle
red	rouge	rouge
green	vert	verte
yellow	jaune	jaune
white	blanc	blanche
black	noir	noire
blue	bleu	bleue

He showed it to Max, who said, "You should also know, sir, that adjectives in French generally follow the **noun**. Just a few common ones – such as 'grand', '**petit**', 'bon', and '**beau**' come before it. 'Une belle voiture bleue' means a beautiful blue car. You must also put an 's' on the adjective if the noun is in the **plural** – 'filles intelligentes' – 'intelligent girls'!"

Ah! So I'm a 'beau monsieur intelligent' and Izzy is 'une belle fille intelligente'.

38

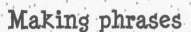

Making phrases

Use these words to make four short descriptions, each four words long. You may use some words more than once. Remember that 'vélo' means 'bike'.

	un	une	grand	grande	
petit	petite	vélo	bleu	bleue	voiture

1 _____

2 _____

3 _____

4 _____

Top Tips!

When you learn new words, learn whether they are masculine or feminine. Then you will always know how to use adjectives with them.

Did you know?

Some French adjectives have different meanings, depending on whether they are in front of or behind the noun. One example is '**propre**'. In front of the noun, it means 'own'. After it, it means 'clean'. So, if you do something with 'mes propres mains propres', you are doing it with your own clean hands.

Sir Ralph goes on and discovers verbs
Sir Ralph continue et découvre les verbes

One Sunday morning at the breakfast table, Sir Ralph looked up from the sports page of his newspaper and muttered, "It's 'e' after 'je', 'ons' after 'nous'. The 'jou' part means 'play'. The bits on the end and the little words in front tell you who's playing."

"Papa! What are you talking about?" said Isabella, puzzled.

"He's talking about 'er' verbs," Max whispered in her ear.

"You see," continued Sir Ralph, speaking more clearly now. "The reporter had asked this young lad if he plays football much. '**Tu joues** au football?' and he'd replied with '**je joue**' – 'I play'. Then his friend told the reporter that they watch all the matches – '**Nous regardons** tous les matchs'. Then the first lad said some nice things about his friend. '**Il joue** très bien' – he plays very well. The reporter then told us where they play every week. '**Ils jouent**' – that means they play – there's 'ent' on the end."

*Mmm.
Je regarde tous les matchs.
Il joue très bien.*

je	regarde	joue
tu	regardes	joues
il	regarde	joue
elle	regarde	joue
nous	regardons	jouons
vous	regardez	jouez
ils	regardent	jouent
elles	regardent	jouent

"Would it be '**elles jouent**' if it were all girls?" asked Isabella.

"That's correct," said Max. "Also, if one girl plays, it would be '**elle joue**'."

"Oh, and look," said Sir Ralph, starting to mutter again as he sometimes did when he was thinking too hard. "Here's how the reporter asked them. '**Vous jouez** toutes les semaines?' – his exact words – 'do you play every week?'" Sir Ralph stared at the paper. "I think I'll just scribble out the verb '**jouer**' so I don't forget it... and '**regarder**', to look; that's an 'er' verb too."

Be a verb detective

Put the words below into the correct slot on this chart.

je regardent elles joue regardes he joue vous
regardez regardons she nous they tu regarde jouent

	WHO	PLAY	WATCH
I	_____	_____	regarde
you (one)	_____	joues	_____
_____	il	_____	regarde
_____	elle	joue	_____
we	_____	jouons	_____
you (more than one)	_____	jouez	_____
_____	ils	_____	regardent
they (all girls)	_____	jouent	_____

Top Tips

'Joue', 'joues' and 'jouent' all sound the same – like
'joo' – even though they are spelt differently.
'Regarde', 'regardes' and 'regardent' also all sound
the same – like the English 'regard'.

Did you know?

Verbs are stored in dictionaries in the **infinitive** form. This is the part of
the verb which means 'to play' or 'to watch'. Even a very big dictionary
could not hold every part of every verb. French infinitives end in 'er', 'ir'
or 're' – look out for those endings when you look up verbs.

Revise Time

1 Unscramble these names of French towns, then put them next to the right description.

zirabrit　　　nacsen　　　snalem　　　jidon　　　nanecy

a　Not far from Switzerland.　　　　　　　_____

b　Famous for mustard.　　　　　　　　　_____

c　On the coast, near Spain.　　　　　　　_____

d　A film festival takes place here each year.　_____

e　Motor racing happens here.　　　　　　_____

2 Put a tick by the statements that are true and a cross by the ones that are false.

a　There are twenty 'départements' in France.　　　　☐

b　The winner of each stage of the Tour de France
　wears a green jersey the next day.　　　　　　　☐

c　The Tour de France came through the Channel Tunnel once.　☐

d　'Il a gagné' means 'He has fallen'.　　　　　　　☐

3 Choose one of these adjectives to complete each sentence.

intelligente　　　important　　　bleue　　　vert　　　grande

a　Le port est　_____　　d　La voiture est　_____

b　La ville est　_____　　e　La fille est　_____

c　Le vélo est　_____

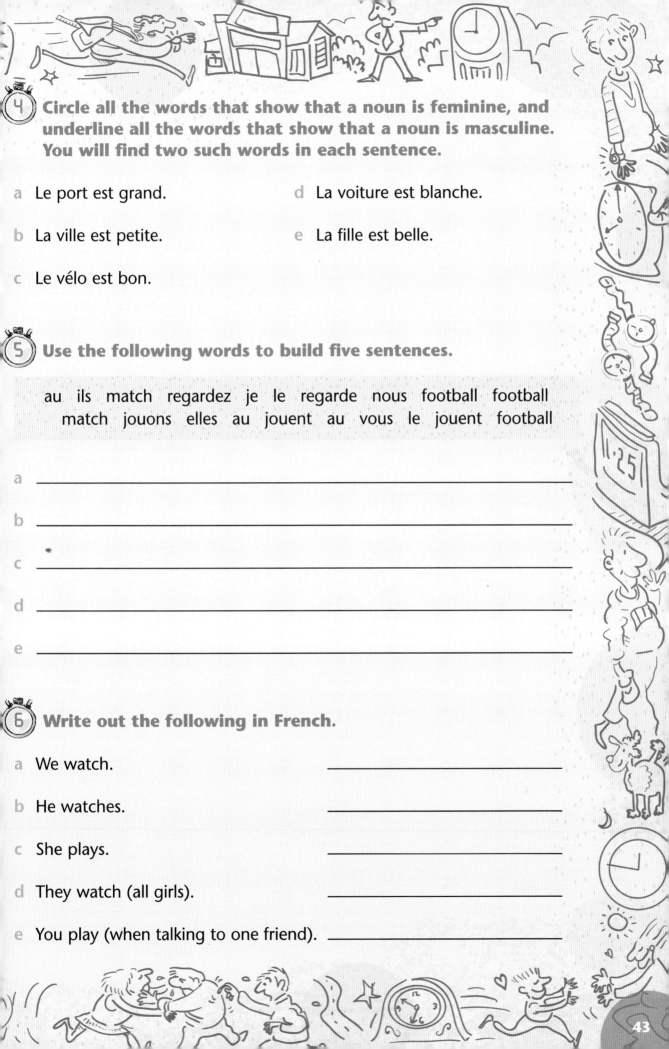

4 Circle all the words that show that a noun is feminine, and underline all the words that show that a noun is masculine. You will find two such words in each sentence.

a Le port est grand.

b La ville est petite.

c Le vélo est bon.

d La voiture est blanche.

e La fille est belle.

5 Use the following words to build five sentences.

au ils match regardez je le regarde nous football football match jouons elles au jouent au vous le jouent football

a _____

b _____

c _____

d _____

e _____

6 Write out the following in French.

a We watch. _____

b He watches. _____

c She plays. _____

d They watch (all girls). _____

e You play (when talking to one friend). _____

Glossary

Afrique (f) Africa
Allemagne (f) Germany
aller to go
Alpes (f pl) Alps
Amérique (f) America
anniversaire (m) birthday
après-midi (m) afternoon
Asie (f) Asia
Atlantique (m) Atlantic
Australie (f) Australia
autobus (m) bus
autruche (f) ostrich

bateau (m) boat
beau/belle beautiful
Belgique (f) Belgium
blanc/blanche white
bon/bonne good

c'est it is / is it?
Canada (m) Canada
cent one hundred
chaîne (f) de montagne
    mountain range
chameau (m) (pl. x)
    camel
cher dear
chez to/in our house
Chine (f) China
cinq five
cinquante fifty
continent (m) continent
cuisine (f) kitchen

de bonne heure bright
    and early
déjeuner (m) lunch
demie half
deux two
dimanche Sunday
dix-huit eighteen

dix-neuf nineteen
dix-sept seventeen
(se) doucher to shower
douze twelve

éléphant (m) elephant
elle she/it
Espagne (f) Spain
est (m) east/is
et demie half past
et quart quarter past
États-Unis (m pl) United
    States
Europe (f) Europe

faire to do/make
fête (f) bank holiday
Fête (f) des Mères
    Mother's Day
Fête (f) Nationale
    National Bank Holiday
Fête (f) du Travail Labour
    Day
fleuve (m) river
France (f) France

gagner to win
Gange (m) Ganges
girafe (f) giraffe
gorille (m) gorilla
Grande-Bretagne (f)
    Great Britain

heure (f) hour/o'clock
Himalaya (m) Himalayas
hippopotame (m)
    hippopotamus
huit eight

il he/it
île (f) island
ils they (all male or
    mixed groups)
Inde (f) India
Italie (f) Italy

Japon (m) Japan
jaune yellow
je I
jeudi Thursday
jouer to play
Jour (m) de l'Ascension
    Ascension Day

kangourou (m) kangaroo

la the (feminine)
le the (masculine)
(se) lever to get up
lion (m) lion
lit (m) bed
Loire (f) the Loire, a river
    in France
lundi Monday

mai May
Manche (f) Channel
mardi Tuesday
Mardi Gras Pancake Day
matin (m) morning
mer (f) sea
mercredi Wednesday
Mercredi des Cendres
    Ash Wednesday
midi noon/lunchtime
minuit midnight
moins le quart quarter to
montagne (f) mountain

nettoyer to clean
neuf nine
Nil (m) Nile
noces (f pl) wedding
Noël Christmas
nord north
nous we
Nouvelle Zélande (f)
    New Zealand
nuit (f) night

océan (m) ocean

oeuf (m) en chocolat chocolate egg

onze eleven

ouest west

ours (m) blanc polar bear

Pacifique (m) Pacific

Pâques Easter

passer l'aspirateur to hoover

pays (m) country

Pays-Bas (m pl) Netherlands

Pentecôte Whitsun

petit small

petit déjeuner (m) breakfast

pied (m) foot

pingouin (m) penguin

port (m) port

premier first

préparer to prepare

propre clean/own

Pyrénées (pl) Pyrenees

quand when

quarante forty

quart quarter (of an hour)

quatorze fourteen

quatre four

quatre-vingts eighty

quatre-vingt-dix ninety

quelle heure est-il? what time is it?

quinze fifteen

randonnée (f) hiking

ranger to tidy

regarder to watch

repassage (m) ironing

retour (m) return

(se) réveiller to wake up

Réveillon meal eaten late on Christmas and New Year's Eve

Rocheuses (f pl) Rockies

rouge red

salle à manger dining room

salle (f) de bains bathroom

salon lounge

samedi Saturday

Scandinavie (f) Scandinavia

Seine (f) the Seine, a French river

seize sixteen

sept seven

serpent (m) snake

singe (m) monkey

six six

soir (m) evening

soixante sixty

soixante-dix seventy

sud south

Suisse (f) Switzerland

Tamise (f) Thames

tigre (m) tiger

toi you

tomber to fall

ton/ta your

tôt early

train (m) train

tramway (m) tram

treize thirteen

trente thirty

trois three

tu you (one person whom you know well)

un a/an/one (masculine)

une a/an/one (feminine)

vaisselle (f) washing up

vélo (m) bike

vendredi Friday

vert green

ville (f) town

voiture (f) car

vous you (more than one person, or one person you do not know well)

zèbre (m) zebra

Adjective A describing word, such as 'blue' or 'small'.

Accent Mark on a letter, which changes a word's pronunciation or meaning.

Feminine/Masculine All French nouns (naming words) are either masculine or feminine. Therefore, instead of saying 'it', you say 'he' ('il') or 'she' ('elle'). It is important to know whether a word is masculine or feminine, so that you know the right word to use for 'the' ('le' or 'la'), 'a' ('un' or 'une'), 'my' ('mon' or 'ma') and 'his' or 'her' ('son' or 'sa').

Irregular verb A verb which does not follow a set pattern.

Infinitive This is the part of the verb which means 'to' .... It always ends in 'er', 'ir' or 're' in French.

Noun A naming word, such as 'table' or 'tiger'.

Plural More than one.

Reflexive verb A verb where the person does the action to themselves.

Verb An action word, such as 'go', 'watch' or 'do'.

Answers

Page 5

a	b	c	d	a	e	f	g	h	i	j	k
l	m	h	o	u	r	s	b	l	a	n	c
o	p	i	q	t	r	s	t	u	v	w	x
y	t	i	g	r	e	i	a	a	b	b	c
l	i	o	n	u	d	n	e	f	f	g	g
z	h	n	j	c	j	g	k	f	t	x	n
m	m	n	o	h	p	e	q	w	e	p	g
z	è	b	r	e	s	t	s	t	u	v	w

Page 7

The first card wins – 30 32 43 47 50 51

Page 9

Noël

Mardi Gras

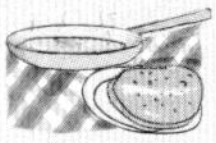

Pâques

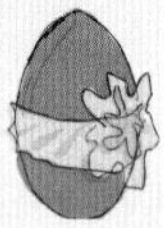

La Fête Nationale

La Fête des Mères

Pages 10–11 Revision exercises

Exercise 1

a S I N G E
b Z È B R E
c L I O N
d O U R S B L A N C
e T I G R E

Exercise 2

a m **b** m **c** f **d** f **e** m

Exercise 3

numbers

a 60 – 52 = 8 (huit)
b 43 – 31 = 12 (douze)
c 50 – 49 = 1 (un)
d 59 – 33 = 26 (vingt-six)
e 49 – 44 = 5 (cinq)

Exercise 4

㉝ 44 55 60 ㉛ 45 56 59 ㉞ ㉜ 46 57 48 (53) 57

Exercise 5

a Noël – December
b La Fête des Mères – May
c La Fête du Travail – May
d La Fête Nationale – July
e Le Jour de l'An – January

Exercise 6

a La Veille de Noël – Christmas Eve
b Pâques – Easter
c Mardi Gras – Pancake Day
d Pentecôte – Whitsun
e Le Jour de l'Ascension – Ascension Day

Page 13

You should have ended on the twenty-second flagstone.

Page 15

Before breakfast – Tôt
Before midday – Le matin
After lunch – L'après-midi
While you're asleep – La nuit
At lunchtime – Midi

Page 17

1 Je passe l'aspirateur
2 Je fais la vaisselle
3 Je fais les lits
4 Je prépare le déjeuner
5 Je range le salon

Pages 18–19 Revision exercises

Exercise 1

a   d

b   e

c

Exercise 2

a faux   b vrai   c faux   d faux

Exercise 3

a de bonne heure   d matin
b midi   e après-midi
c soir

Exercise 4

a tôt   d après-midi
b matin   e soir
c midi

Exercise 5

a Je me réveille
b Je me lève
c Je me douche
d Je prépare le petit déjeuner
e Je fais la vaisselle

Exercise 6

Je passe l'aspirateur.

Je prépare le déjeuner.

Je fais le repassage.

Je nettoie la salle de bains.

Je fais les lits.

Page 21

89 90 91

Page 23

Pierre – the 15th of September
Paulette – the 30th of August
Armelle – the 25th of November
Alexandre – the 10th of March
Yvette – the 29th of May

Page 25

1 Afrique   4 Canada
2 Rocheuses   5 Atlantique
3 France   6 Gange

Pages 26–27 Revision exercises

Exercise 1

dix-sept, dix-huit, soixante-sept, soixante-huit, soixante-dix, soixante-dix-sept, soixante-dix-huit, quatre-vingt-dix-sept, quatre-vingt-dix-huit

Exercise 2

a soixante-quatorze – 74
b soixante-cinq – 65
c quatre-vingts – 80
d quatre-vingt-dix-neuf – 99
e quatre-vingt-trois – 83

Exercise 3

a It is their saint's day. They have a name, which they share with a saint. On his or her day, they celebrate.
b Bon anniversaire
c When's your birthday?
d Chère Izzy

Exercise 4

mars avril juin janvier novembre

Exercise 5

Atlantique

Exercise 6

a Espagne   d Amérique
b Atlantique   e Gange
c Manche

Page 29

Verticalement: **1** mercredi **3** Italie
Horizontalement: **2** par le train
4 bateau **5** avion

Page 31

je vais, tu vas, il va, elle va, nous allons, vous allez, ils vont, elles vont

Page 33

Marseille est une grande ville dans le sud de la France.

Pages 34–35 Revision exercises

Exercise 1
You use 'en' with bateau, avion, tramway, autobus and voiture.
You use 'à' with the rest.

Exercise 2
a lundi
b jeudi
c vendredi
d mercredi
e samedi

Exercise 3
a je vais
b il va
c vous allez
d nous allons
e elles vont

Exercise 4
a You are going
b She is going
c We are going
d They are going
e I am going

Exercise 5
You should have crossed out:
a 'un port important' 'le sud' and 'l'Angleterre'
b 'une grande ville' 'le nord-est' and l'Angleterre'. Manchester est une grande ville dans le nord de l'Angleterre.

Exercise 6
a montagne
b sud
c port
d fleuve
e océan

Page 37

capital – Paris
mustard – Dijon
champagne – Châlons-en-Champagne
films – Cannes
seaside resort – Biarritz

Page 39

un grand vélo bleu
un petit vélo bleu
une grande voiture bleue
une petite voiture bleue

Page 41

	who	play	watch
I	je	joue	regarde
you (one)	tu	joues	regardes
he	il	joue	regarde
she	elle	joue	regarde
we	nous	jouons	regardons
you (more than one)	vous	jouez	regardez
they	ils	jouent	regardent
they (all girls)	elles	jouent	regardent

Pages 42–43 Revision exercises

Exercise 1
a Annecy
b Dijon
c Biarritz
d Cannes
e Le Mans

Exercise 2
a ✘ **b** ✘ **c** ✔ **d** ✘

Exercise 3
a important
b grande
c vert
d bleue
e intelligente

Exercise 4
a Le port est grand.
b La ville est petite.
c Le vélo est bon.
d La voiture est blanche.
e La fille est belle.

Exercise 5
a Je regarde le match.
b Nous jouons au football.
c Elles jouent au football.
d Ils jouent au football.
e Vous regardez le match.

Exercise 6
a Nous regardons
b Il regarde
c Elle joue
d Elles regardent
e Tu joues